Turtle Island

OTHER BOOKS BY GARY SNYDER

TURTLE ISLAND

Gary Snyder

A New Directions Book

ACKNOWLEDGMENTS
Grateful acknowledgment is made to the editors and publishers of various publications in which some of the material in this book first appeared: *Aldebaran, Caterpillar, City Lights Journal, Clear Creek, Copper Canyon, Crazy Horse, Fiction International, The Hudson Review, Hyperion, Jeopardy, Kayak, Kuksu, Look, Marijuana Review, New American Review, New Directions in Prose and Poetry, The New York Times, Not Man Apart, North Country, Organ, Peace & Pieces, Raster, Rising Generation, Rogue River Gorge, Unmuzzled Ox, World.*

The section "Manzanita" was originally brought out in a limited edition by the Four Seasons Foundation (Bolinas, California) in 1972. "The Hudsonian Curlew" first appeared in *Poetry.*

Manufactured in the United States of America
First published clothbound and as New Directions Paperbook 381 in 1974
Published simultaneously in Canada by McClelland & Stewart, Ltd.

Library of Congress Cataloging in Publication Data

Snyder, Gary.
    Turtle Island.

    (A New Directions Book)
    Poems.
    I. Title.
PS3569.N88T8   811'.5'4   74–8542
ISBN 0–8112–0545–2
ISBN 0–8112–0546–0 (pbk.)

New Directions Books are published for James Laughlin
by New Directions Publishing Corporation,
333 Sixth Avenue, New York 10014

SECOND PRINTING

CONTENTS

MANZANITA

MAGPIE'S SONG

FOR THE CHILDREN

PLAIN TALK

FOR LOIS SNYDER HENNESSY
MY MOTHER

INTRODUCTORY NOTE

Turtle Island—the old/new name for the continent, based on many creation myths of the people who have been living here for millenia, and reapplied by some of them to "North America" in recent years. Also, an idea found world-wide, of the earth, or cosmos even, sustained by a great turtle or serpent-of-eternity.

A name: that we may see ourselves more accurately on this continent of watersheds and life-communities—plant zones, physiographic provinces, culture areas; following natural boundaries. The "U.S.A." and its states and counties are arbitrary and inaccurate impositions on what is really here.

The poems speak of place, and the energy-pathways that sustain life. Each living being is a swirl in the flow, a formal turbulence, a "song." The land, the planet itself, is also a living being—at another pace. Anglos, Black people, Chicanos, and others beached up on these shores all share such views at the deepest levels of their old cultural traditions—African, Asian, or European. Hark again to those roots, to see our ancient solidarity, and then to the work of being together on Turtle Island.

MANZANITA

ANASAZI

Anasazi,
Anasazi,

tucked up in clefts in the cliffs
growing strict fields of corn and beans
sinking deeper and deeper in earth
up to your hips in Gods
    your head all turned to eagle-down
    & lightning for knees and elbows
your eyes full of pollen

   the smell of bats.
   the flavor of sandstone
   grit on the tongue.

   women
   birthing
at the foot of ladders in the dark.

trickling streams in hidden canyons
under the cold rolling desert

corn-basket   wide-eyed
   red baby
   rock lip home,

Anasazi

THE WAY WEST, UNDERGROUND

The split-cedar
smoked salmon
cloudy days of Oregon,
the thick fir forests.

       Black Bear heads uphill in
       Plumas county,
       round bottom scuttling through willows—

The Bear Wife moves up the coast.

       where blackberry brambles
       ramble in the burns.

And around the curve of islands
foggy volcanoes
on, to North Japan. The bears
& fish-spears of the Ainu.
Gilyak.
Mushroom-vision healer,
single flat drum,
from long before China.

Women with drums who fly over Tibet.

Following forests west, and
rolling, following grassland,
tracking bears and mushrooms,
eating berries all the way.
In Finland finally took a bath:
       like redwood sweatlodge on the Klamath—
all the Finns in moccasins and
pointy hats with dots of white,

netting, trapping, bathing,
singing holding hands, the while

see-sawing on a bench, a look of love—

Karhu—Bjorn—Braun—Bear

      [lightning rainbow great cloud tree
          dialogs of birds]
Europa.   'The West.'
the bears are gone
        except Brunhilde?

or elder wilder goddesses reborn—will race
   the streets of France and Spain
      with automatic guns—
      in Spain,
Bears and Bison,
Red Hands with missing fingers,
Red mushroom labyrinths;
lightning-bolt mazes,
Painted in caves,

Underground.

WITHOUT

the silence

of nature

within.

the power within.

the power

without.

the path is whatever passes—no

end in itself.

the end is,

grace—ease—

healing,

not saving.

singing

the proof

the proof of the power within.

THE DEAD BY THE SIDE OF THE ROAD

How did a great Red-tailed Hawk
   come to lie—all stiff and dry—
      on the shoulder of
         Interstate 5?

Her wings for dance fans

Zac skinned a skunk with a crushed head
   washed the pelt in gas; it hangs,
      tanned, in his tent

Fawn stew on Hallowe'en
   hit by a truck on highway forty-nine
      offer cornmeal by the mouth;
         skin it out.

Log trucks run on fossil fuel

I never saw a Ringtail til I found one in the road:
   case-skinned it with the toenails
      footpads, nose, and whiskers on;
         it soaks in salt and water
         sulphuric acid pickle;

she will be a pouch for magic tools.

The Doe was apparently shot
   lengthwise and through the side—
      shoulder and out the flank
         belly full of blood

Can save the other shoulder maybe,
   if she didn't lie too long—
Pray to their spirits. Ask them to bless us:
   our ancient sisters' trails
      the roads were laid across and kill them:
         night-shining eyes

The dead by the side of the road.

I WENT INTO THE MAVERICK BAR

I went into the Maverick Bar
In Farmington, New Mexico.
And drank double shots of bourbon
                    backed with beer.
My long hair was tucked up under a cap
I'd left the earring in the car.

Two cowboys did horseplay
                    by the pool tables,
A waitress asked us
                    where are you from?
a country-and-western band began to play
"We don't smoke Marijuana in Muskokie"
And with the next song,
                    a couple began to dance.

They held each other like in High School dances
                    in the fifties;
I recalled when I worked in the woods
                    and the bars of Madras, Oregon.
That short-haired joy and roughness—
                    America—your stupidity.
I could almost love you again.

We left—onto the freeway shoulders—
                    under the tough old stars—
In the shadow of bluffs
                    I came back to myself,
To the real work, to
                    "What is to be done."

STEAK

Up on the bluff, the steak houses
called "The Embers"—called
"Fireside"
with a smiling disney cow on the sign
or a stockman's pride—huge
full-color photo of standing Hereford stud
above the very booth
his bloody sliced muscle is
       served in;
       "rare"

The Chamber of Commerce eats there,
the visiting lecturer,
stockmen in Denver suits,
Japanese-American animal nutrition experts
       from Kansas,
       with Buddhist beads;

And down by the tracks
in frozen mud, in the feed lots,
fed surplus grain
(the ripped-off land)
the beeves are standing round—
bred heavy.
Steaming, stamping,
long-lashed, slowly thinking
with the rhythm of their
breathing,
frosty—breezy—
early morning prairie sky.

NO MATTER, NEVER MIND

The Father is the Void
The Wife   Waves

Their child is Matter.

Matter makes it with his mother
And their child is Life,
                    a daughter.

The Daughter is the Great Mother
Who, with her father/brother Matter
                  as her lover,

Gives birth to the Mind.

THE BATH

Washing Kai in the sauna,
The kerosene lantern set on a box
    outside the ground-level window,
Lights up the edge of the iron stove and the
    washtub down on the slab
Steaming air and crackle of waterdrops
    brushed by on the pile of rocks on top
He stands in warm water
Soap all over the smooth of his thigh and stomach
    "Gary don't soap my hair!"
    —his eye-sting fear—
    the soapy hand feeling
    through and around the globes and curves of his body
    up in the crotch,
And washing-tickling out the scrotum, little anus,
    his penis curving up and getting hard
    as I pull back skin and try to wash it
Laughing and jumping, flinging arms around,
    I squat all naked too,
                is this our body?

Sweating and panting in the stove-steam hot-stone
    cedar-planking wooden bucket water-splashing
    kerosene lantern-flicker wind-in-the-pines-out
    sierra forest ridges night—
Masa comes in, letting fresh cool air
    sweep down from the door
    a deep sweet breath
And she tips him over gripping neatly, one knee down
    her hair falling hiding one whole side of
    shoulder, breast, and belly,
Washes deftly Kai's head-hair
    as he gets mad and yells—
The body of my lady, the winding valley spine,

12

the space between the thighs I reach through,
cup her curving vulva arch and hold it from behind,
a soapy tickle   a hand of grail
The gates of Awe
That open back a turning double-mirror world of
wombs in wombs, in rings,
that start in music,
                         is this our body?

The hidden place of seed
The veins net flow across the ribs, that gathers
milk and peaks up in a nipple—fits
our mouth—
The sucking milk from this our body sends through
jolts of light; the son, the father,
sharing mother's joy
That brings a softness to the flower of the awesome
open curling lotus gate I cup and kiss
As Kai laughs at his mother's breast he now is weaned
from, we
wash each other,
                         this our body

Kai's little scrotum up close to his groin,
the seed still tucked away, that moved from us to him
In flows that lifted with the same joys forces
as his nursing Masa later,
playing with her breast,
Or me within her,
Or him emerging,
                         this is our body:

Clean, and rinsed, and sweating more, we stretch
out on the redwood benches hearts all beating
Quiet to the simmer of the stove,
the scent of cedar
And then turn over,

murmuring gossip of the grasses,
talking firewood,
Wondering how Gen's napping, how to bring him in
soon wash him too—
These boys who love their mother
who loves men, who passes on
her sons to other women;

The cloud across the sky. The windy pines.
the trickle gurgle in the swampy meadow

this is our body.

Fire inside and boiling water on the stove
We sigh and slide ourselves down from the benches
wrap the babies, step outside,

black night & all the stars.

Pour cold water on the back and thighs
Go in the house—stand steaming by the center fire
Kai scampers on the sheepskin
Gen standing hanging on and shouting,

"Bao! bao! bao! bao! bao!"

This is our body. Drawn up crosslegged by the flames
drinking icy water
hugging babies, kissing bellies,

Laughing on the Great Earth

Come out from the bath.

COYOTE VALLEY SPRING

Cubs
tumble in the damp leaves
Deer, bear, squirrel.
fresh winds scour the
spring stars.
rocks crumble
deep mud hardens
under heavy hills.

shifting things
birds, weeds,
slip through the air
through eyes and ears,

Coyote valley. *Olema*
in the spring.
white and solemn toloache flower

and far out in the *tamal*
a lost people
float

in tiny tule boats.

SPEL AGAINST DEMONS

The release of Demonic Energies in the name of
                                        the People
                    must cease

Messing with blood sacrifice in the name of
                                        Nature
                    must cease

The stifling self-indulgence in anger in the name of
                                        Freedom
                    must cease

this is death to clarity
death to compassion

the man who has the soul of the wolf
knows the self-restraint
of the wolf

aimless executions and slaughterings
are not the work of wolves and eagles

but the work of hysterical sheep

The Demonic must be devoured!
Self-serving must be
                    cut down
Anger must be
                    plowed back
Fearlessness, humor, detachment, is power

Gnowledge is the secret of Transformation!

Down with demonic killers who mouth revolutionary
slogans and muddy the flow of change, may they be
Bound by the Noose, and Instructed by the Diamond
Sword of ACHALA the Immovable, Lord of Wisdom, Lord
of Heat, who is squint-eyed and whose face is terrible
with bare fangs, who wears on his crown a garland of
severed heads, clad in a tiger skin, he who turns
Wrath to Purified Accomplishment,

> whose powers are of lava,
> of magma, of deep rock strata, of gunpowder,
> and the Sun.

He who saves tortured intelligent demons and filth-eating
hungry ghosts, his spel is,

NAMAH SAMANTAH VAJRANAM CHANDA
  MAHAROSHANA
        SPHATAYA HUM TRAKA HAM MAM

FRONT LINES

The edge of the cancer
Swells against the hill—we feel
          a foul breeze—
And it sinks back down.
The deer winter here
A chainsaw growls in the gorge.

Ten wet days and the log trucks stop,
The trees breathe.
Sunday the 4-wheel jeep of the
Realty Company brings in
Landseekers, lookers, they say
To the land,
Spread your legs.

The jets crack sound overhead, it's OK here;
Every pulse of the rot at the heart
In the sick fat veins of Amerika
Pushes the edge up closer—

A bulldozer grinding and slobbering
Sideslipping and belching on top of
The skinned-up bodies of still-live bushes
In the pay of a man
From town.

Behind is a forest that goes to the Arctic
And a desert that still belongs to the Piute
And here we must draw
Our line.

CONTROL BURN

What the Indians
here
used to do, was,
to burn out the brush every year.
in the woods, up the gorges,
keeping the oak and the pine stands
tall and clear
with grasses
and kitkitdizze under them,
never enough fuel there
that a fire could crown.

Now, manzanita,
(a fine bush in its right)
crowds up under the new trees
mixed up with logging slash
and a fire can wipe out all.

Fire is an old story.
I would like,
with a sense of helpful order,
with respect for laws
of nature,
to help my land
with a burn. a hot clean
burn.
       (manzanita seeds will only open
       after a fire passes over
       or once passed through a bear)

And then
it would be more
like,
when it belonged to the Indians

Before.

THE GREAT MOTHER

Not all those who pass

In front of the Great Mother's chair

Get passt with only a stare.

Some she looks at their hands

To see what sort of savages they were.

THE CALL OF THE WILD

✳

The heavy old man in his bed at night
Hears the Coyote singing
                    in the back meadow.
All the years he ranched and mined and logged.
A Catholic.
A native Californian.
          and the Coyotes howl in his
Eightieth year.
He will call the Government
Trapper
Who uses iron leg-traps on Coyotes,
Tomorrow.
My sons will lose this
Music they have just started
To love.

✳

The ex acid-heads from the cities
Converted to Guru or Swami,
Do penance with shiny
Dopey eyes, and quit eating meat.
In the forests of North America,
The land of Coyote and Eagle,
They dream of India, of
          forever blissful sexless highs.
And sleep in oil-heated
Geodesic domes, that
Were stuck like warts
In the woods.

And the Coyote singing
    is shut away
    for they fear
    the call
    of the wild.

And they sold their virgin cedar trees,
    the tallest trees in miles,
To a logger
Who told them,

"Trees are full of bugs."

❋

The Government finally decided
To wage the war   all-out. Defeat
    is Un-American.
And they took to the air,
Their women beside them
    in bouffant hairdos
    putting nail-polish on the
    gunship cannon-buttons.
And they never came down,
    for they found,
    the ground
is pro-Communist. And dirty.
And the insects side with the Viet Cong.

So they bomb and they bomb
Day after day, across the planet
    blinding sparrows
    breaking the ear-drums of owls
    splintering trunks of cherries
    twining and looping
    deer intestines
    in the shaken, dusty, rocks.

All these Americans up in special cities in the sky
Dumping poisons and explosives
Across Asia first,
And next North America,

A war against earth.
When it's done there'll be
        no place

A Coyote could hide.

                    envoy

            I would like to say
            Coyote is forever
            Inside you.

            But it's not true.

PRAYER FOR THE GREAT FAMILY

Gratitude to Mother Earth, sailing through night and day—
    and to her soil: rich, rare, and sweet
        in our minds so be it.

Gratitude to Plants, the sun-facing light-changing leaf
    and fine root-hairs; standing still through wind
    and rain; their dance is in the flowing spiral grain
        in our minds so be it.

Gratitude to Air, bearing the soaring Swift and the silent
    Owl at dawn. Breath of our song
    clear spirit breeze
        in our minds so be it.

Gratitude to Wild Beings, our brothers, teaching secrets,
    freedoms, and ways; who share with us their milk;
    self-complete, brave, and aware
        in our minds so be it.

Gratitude to Water: clouds, lakes, rivers, glaciers;
    holding or releasing; streaming through all
    our bodies salty seas
        in our minds so be it.

Gratitude to the Sun: blinding pulsing light through
    trunks of trees, through mists, warming caves where
    bears and snakes sleep—he who wakes us—
        in our minds so be it.

Gratitude to the Great Sky
   who holds billions of stars—and goes yet beyond that—
   beyond all powers, and thoughts
   and yet is within us—
   Grandfather Space.
   The Mind is his Wife.

       so be it.

                       after a Mohawk prayer

SOURCE

To be in
to the land
where croppt-out rock
can hardly see
the swiftly passing trees

Manzanita clans
cluster up and fan out on their soils
in streaks and sweeps
with birds and woodrats underneath

And clay swale keeps wet,
free of trees, the bunch-grass
like no Spaniard ever came

I hear no news

Cloud finger dragons dance and
tremble down the ridge
and spit and spiral snow then pull in
quivering, on the sawtooth
spine

Clears up, and all the stars.
the tree leaves catch
some extra tiny source
all the wide night

Up here
out back
drink deep
that black light.

MANZANITA

Before dawn the coyotes
    weave medicine songs
    dream nets—spirit baskets—
    milky way music
        they cook young girls with
        to be woman;
  or the whirling dance of
  striped boys—

At moon-set the pines are gold-purple
Just before sunrise.

The dog hastens into the undergrowth
Comes back panting
Huge, on the small dry flowers.

A woodpecker
Drums and echoes
Across the still meadow

One man draws, and releases   an arrow
Humming, flat,
Missing a gray stump, and splitting
A smooth red twisty manzanita bough.

Manzanita   the tips in fruit,
Clusters of hard green berries
The longer you look
The bigger they seem,

      "little apples"

CHARMS

for Michael McClure

The beauty of naked or half-naked women,
lying in nothing clear or obvious—not
in exposure; but a curve of the back or arm,
as a dance or—evoking "another world"

"The Deva Realm" or better, the Delight
at the heart of creation.

Brought out for each mammal species
specifically—in some dreamlike perfection
of name-and-form

Thus I could be devastated and athirst with longing
for a lovely mare or lioness, or lady mouse,
in seeing the beauty from THERE
shining through her, some toss of the whiskers
or grace-full wave of the tail

that enchants.

enchants, and thus

CHARMS.

MAGPIE'S SONG

FACTS

1. 92% of Japan's three million ton import of soybeans comes from the U.S.

2. The U.S. has 6% of the world's population; consumes 1/3 the energy annually consumed in the world.

3. The U.S. consumes 1/3 of the world's annual meat.

4. The top 1/5 of American population gets 45% of salary income, and owns about 77% of the total wealth. The top 1% owns 20 to 30% of personal wealth.

5. A modern nation needs 13 basic industrial raw materials. By AD 2000 the U.S. will be import-dependent on all but phosphorus.

6. General Motors is bigger than Holland.

7. Nuclear energy is mainly subsidized with fossil fuels and barely yields net energy.

8. The "Seven Sisters"—Exxon, Mobil, Texaco, Gulf, Standard of California, British Petroleum, Royal Dutch Shell.

9. "The reason solar energy has not and will not be a major contributor or substitute for fossil fuels is that it will not compete without energy subsidy from fossil fuel economy. The plants have already maximized the use of sunlight."—H. T. Odum

10. Our primary source of food is the sun.

THE REAL WORK

[*Today with Zach & Dan rowing by Alcatraz and around Angel Island*]

sea-lions and birds,
sun through fog
flaps up and lolling,
looks you dead in the eye.
sun haze;
a long tanker riding light and high.

sharp wave choppy line—
interface tide-flows—
seagulls sit on the meeting
eating;
we slide by white-stained cliffs.

the real work.
washing and sighing,
sliding by.

PINE TREE TOPS,

in the blue night
frost haze, the sky glows
with the moon
pine tree tops
bend snow-blue, fade
into sky, frost, starlight.
the creak of boots.
rabbit tracks, deer tracks,
what do we know.

FOR NOTHING

Earth a flower
A phlox on the steep
slopes of light
hanging over the vast
solid spaces
small rotten crystals;
salts.

Earth a flower
by a gulf where a raven
flaps by once
a glimmer, a color
forgotten as all
falls away.

A flower
for nothing;
an offer;
no taker;

Snow-trickle, feldspar, dirt.

NIGHT HERONS

Night herons nest in the cypress
by the San Francisco
stationary boilers
with the high smoke stack
at the edge of the waters:
a steam turbine pump
to drive salt water
into the city's veins
mains
if the earth ever
quakes. and the power fails.
and water
to fight fire, runs
loose on the streets
with no pressure.

At the wire gate tilted slightly out
the part-wolf dog
would go in, to follow
if his human buddy lay on his side
and squirmed up first.

An abandoned, decaying, army.
a rotten rusty island prison
surrounded by lights of whirling
fluttering god-like birds
who truth
has never forgot.

I walk with my wife's sister
past the frozen bait;
with a long-bearded architect,
my dear brother,
and silent friend, whose

mustache curves wetly into his mouth
and he sometimes bites it.

the dog knows no laws and is strictly,
illegal. His neck arches and ears prick out
to catch mice in the tundra.
a black high school boy
drinking coffee at a fake green stand
tries to be friends with the dog,
and it works.

How could the
night herons ever come back?
to this noisy place on the bay.
like me.
the joy of all the beings
is in being
older and tougher and eaten
up.
in the tubes and lanes of things
in the sewers of bliss and judgment,
in the glorious cleansing
treatment
plants.

We pick our way
through the edge of the city
early
subtly spreading changing sky;

ever-fresh and lovely dawn.

THE EGG

"A snake-like beauty in the living changes of syntax"
—Robert Duncan

Kai twists
rubs "bellybutton"
rubs skin, front and back
two legs kicking
anus a sensitive center
     the pull-together
     between there and the scrotum,
the center line,
with the out-flyers changing
—fins, legs, wings,
feathers or fur,
they swing and swim
but the snake center
fire pushes through:
     mouth to ass,
     root to
     burning, steady,
     single eye.

breeze in the brown grasses
high clouds deep
blue.   white.
blue.   moving
changing

my Mother's old
soft arm. walking
helping up the
path.

Kai's hand
in my fist

the neck bones,
a little thread,
a garland,
of consonants and vowels
from the third eye
through the body's flowers
a string of peaks,
a whirlpool
sucking to the root.

It all gathers,
humming,
in the egg.

THE USES OF LIGHT

It warms my bones
    say the stones

I take it into me and grow
Say the trees
Leaves above
Roots below

A vast vague white
Draws me out of the night
Says the moth in his flight—

Some things I smell
Some things I hear
And I see things move
Says the deer—

A high tower
on a wide plain.
If you climb up
One floor
You'll see a thousand miles more.

ON SAN GABRIEL RIDGES

I dream of—
soft, white, washable country
clothes.
woven zones.
scats
up here on the rocks;
seeds, stickers, twigs, bits of grass
on my belly, pressed designs—

O loves of long ago
          hello again.
all of us together
with all our other loves and children
twining and knotting
through each other—
intricate, chaotic, done.
I dive with you all
and it curls back, freezes;
the laws of waves.
as clear as a canyon wall
as sweet,
as long ago.

woven
into the dark.
squirrel hairs,
squirrel bones crunched,
tight and dry in scats of
fox.

BY FRAZIER CREEK FALLS.

Standing up on lifted, folded rock
looking out and down—

The creek falls to a far valley.
hills beyond that
facing, half-forested, dry
—clear sky
strong wind in the
stiff glittering needle clusters
of the pine—their brown
round trunk bodies
straight, still;
rustling trembling limbs and twigs

listen.

This living flowing land
is all there is, forever

We *are* it
it sings through us—

We could live on this Earth
without clothes or tools!

BLACK MESA MINE #1

Wind dust yellow cloud swirls
northeast across the fifty-foot
graded bulldozed road,
white cloud puffs,
juniper and pinyon scattered groves
        —firewood for the People
            heaps of wood for all
            at cross-streets in the pueblos,
ancient mother mountain
pools of water
pools of coal
pools of sand
                buried or laid bare

Solitary trucks go slow on grades
smoking sand
writhes around the tires
and on a torn up stony plain
a giant green-and-yellow shovel
whirs and drags
house-size scoops of rock and gravel

Mountain,
be kind,
it will tumble in its hole

Five hundred yards   back up the road
a Navajo corral
of stood up dried out poles and logs
all leaned in on an angle,
gleaming in the windy April sun.

UP BRANCHES OF DUCK RIVER

Shaka valley—chickens thousands
                    murmur in sheet walls
past plaster house of welder-sculptor
                    shakuhachi pond,
dead grass golf-course bulldozed on the hill
                    pine Dragon Benten
ridgetop—far off Kyoto on the flat,
turn in to deeper hills toward himuru, "Ice House"—
cut-back Sugi—logger shelter—

Low pass, a snow patch still up here,
they once stored ice for summer,
old women stoking bath fire
white plum bloom

Old man burning brush, a wood sheath for the saw

Over the edge & down to Kamo River
white hills—Mt. Hiei, Hira—cut clean
reseed patchwork, orchard fir

Muddy slipping trail
wobbly twin pole bridges
                gully throat
         forks in
somebody clearing brush & growing tea
& out, turn here for home
along the Kamo River.

hold it close
give it all away.

IT PLEASES

Far above the dome
Of the capitol—
        It's true!
A large bird soars
Against white cloud,
Wings arced,
Sailing easy in this
humid Southern sun-blurred
        breeze—
      the dark-suited policeman
      watches tourist cars—

And the center,
The center of power is nothing!
Nothing here.
Old white stone domes,
Strangely quiet people,

Earth-sky-bird patterns
        idly interlacing

The world does what it pleases.

Washington D.C. XI:73

44

HEMP

for Michael Aldritch

Gravel-bars, riverbanks, scars
of the glaciers,
healing and nursing moraine—
tall hemp plants followed man

      midden   dump heap   roadway slash

To bind his loads and ease his mind
      Moor to Spain, Spain in horse-manure
      and straw, across the sea
      & up from Mexico

—a tiny puff of white cloud far away.
we sit and wait, for days,
and pray for rain.

THE WILD MUSHROOM

Well the sunset rays are shining
Me and Kai have got our tools
A basket and a trowel
And a book with all the rules

Don't ever eat Boletus
If the tube-mouths they are red
Stay away from the Amanitas
Or brother you are dead

Sometimes they're already rotten
Or the stalks are broken off
Where the deer have knocked them over
While turning up the duff

We set out in the forest
To seek the wild mushroom
In shapes diverse and colorful
Shining through the woodland gloom

If you look out under oak trees
Or around an old pine stump
You'll know a mushroom's coming
By the way the leaves are humped

They send out multiple fibers
Through the roots and sod
Some make you mighty sick they say
Or bring you close to God

So here's to the mushroom family
A far-flung friendly clan
For food, for fun, for poison
They are a help to man.

MOTHER EARTH: HER WHALES

An owl winks in the shadows
A lizard lifts on tiptoe, breathing hard
Young male sparrow stretches up his neck,
            big head, watching—

The grasses are working in the sun. Turn it green.
Turn it sweet. That we may eat.
Grow our meat.

Brazil says "sovereign use of Natural Resources"
Thirty thousand kinds of unknown plants.
The living actual people of the jungle
            sold and tortured—
And a robot in a suit who peddles a delusion called "Brazil"
            can speak for *them?*

            The whales turn and glisten, plunge
                        and sound and rise again,
            Hanging over subtly darkening deeps
            Flowing like breathing planets
                        in the sparkling whorls of
                                    living light—

And Japan quibbles for words on
            what kinds of whales they can kill?
A once-great Buddhist nation
            dribbles methyl mercury
            like gonorrhea
                        in the sea.

Père David's Deer, the Elaphure,
Lived in the tule marshes of the Yellow River
Two thousand years ago—and lost its home to rice—
The forests of Lo-yang were logged and all the silt &
Sand flowed down, and gone, by 1200 AD—

Wild Geese hatched out in Siberia
                    head south over basins of the Yang, the Huang,
          what we call "China"
On flyways they have used a million years.
Ah China, where are the tigers, the wild boars,
          the monkeys,
                    like the snows of yesteryear
Gone in a mist, a flash, and the dry hard ground
Is parking space for fifty thousand trucks.
IS man most precious of all things?
—then let us love him, and his brothers, all those
Fading living beings—

North America, Turtle Island, taken by invaders
          who wage war around the world.
May ants, may abalone, otters, wolves and elk
Rise! and pull away their giving
          from the robot nations.

Solidarity. The People.
Standing Tree People!
Flying Bird People!
Swimming Sea People!
Four-legged, two-legged, people!

How can the head-heavy power-hungry politic scientist
Government   two-world   Capitalist-Imperialist
Third-world   Communist   paper-shuffling male
          non-farmer   jet-set   bureaucrats
Speak for the green of the leaf? Speak for the soil?

(Ah Margaret Mead . . . do you sometimes dream of Samoa?)

The robots argue how to parcel out our Mother Earth
To last a little longer
                    like vultures flapping
Belching, gurgling,
                    near a dying Doe.

"In yonder field a slain knight lies—
We'll fly to him and eat his eyes
                with a down
     derry derry derry down down."

          An Owl winks in the shadow
          A lizard lifts on tiptoe
                    breathing hard
          The whales turn and glisten
                    plunge and
          Sound, and rise again
          Flowing like breathing planets

          In the sparkling whorls

          Of living light.

Stockholm: Summer Solstice 40072

AFFLUENCE

under damp layers of pine needle
still-hard limbs and twigs
tangled as they lay,
two sixteen foot good butt logs took
all the rest, top, left

and this from logging twenty years ago
(figured from core-ring reading on a tree
still stands, hard by a stump)
they didn't pile the slash and burn then—

fire hazard, every summer day.

it was the logger's cost
at lumber's going rate then

now burn the tangles dowsing
pokey heaps with diesel oil.
paying the price somebody didn't pay.

.

ETHNOBOTANY

In June two oak fell,
rot in the roots

Chainsaw in September
in three days one tree
bucked and quartered in the shed

sour fresh inner oak-wood smell
the main trunk splits
"like opening a book" (J. Tecklin)

And slightly humping oak leaves
deer muzzle and kick it,
Boletus.
one sort, *Alice Eastwood*
pink, and poison;

Two yellow. *edulus*
"edible and choice."
only I got just so slightly sick—

Taste all, and hand the knowledge down.

STRAIGHT-CREEK—GREAT BURN

for Tom and Martha Burch

Lightly, in the April mountains—
        Straight Creek,
dry grass freed again of snow
& the chickadees are pecking
last fall's seeds
        fluffing tail in chilly wind,

Avalanche piled up cross the creek
        and chunked-froze solid—
water sluicing under; spills out
        rock lip pool, bends over,
        braided, white, foaming,
returns to trembling
        deep-dark hole.

Creek boulders show the flow-wear lines
        in shapes the same
        as running blood
        carves in the heart's main
        valve,

Early spring dry. Dry snow flurries;
        walk on crusty high snow slopes
—grand dead burn pine—
        chartreuse lichen as adornment
        (a dye for wool)
angled tumbled talus rock
of geosyncline warm sea bottom
yes, so long ago.
"Once on a time."

Far light on the Bitteroots;
      scrabble down willow slide
changing clouds above,
shapes on glowing sun-ball
writing,   choosing
      reaching out against eternal
                azure—

us resting on dry fern and
      watching

Shining Heaven
change his feather garments
    overhead.

A whoosh of birds
swoops up and round
tilts back
almost always flying all apart
and yet hangs on!
together;

never a leader,
all of one swift

empty
dancing   mind.

They arc and loop & then
their flight is done.
they settle down.
end of poem.

THE HUDSONIAN CURLEW

for Drum and Diana

The end of a desert track–turnaround–
      parked the truck and walked over dunes.
a cobbly point   hooks in the shallow bay;

            the Mandala of Birds.

pelican, seagulls, and terns,
            one curlew
            far at the end–
they fly up as they see us
                        and settle back down.
tern keep coming
                        –skies of wide seas–
frigate birds keep swooping

pelicans sit nearest the foam;

tern bathing and fluttering
            in frothy wave-lapping
                        between the round stones.

            we
gather driftwood for firewood
for camping
get four shells to serve up steamed snail

            in the top of the cardón cactus
            two vultures
            look, yawn, hunch, preen.
            out on the point   the seabirds
            squabble and settle, meet and leave;
                        speak.

two sides of a border.
the margins.   tidewater.   zones.
up in the void,   under the surface,
two worlds   touch
and greet

❋

Three shotgun shots as it gets dark;
two birds.
> *"how come three shots?"*
> *"one went down on the water*
> *and started to swim.*
> *I didn't want another thing like that duck."*

the bill curved in, and the long neck limp—
a grandmother plumage of cinnamon and brown.
the beak not so long—bars on the head;
          by the eye.
          Hudsonian Curlew

               and those tern most likely
               "Royal Tern"
               with forked tail,
               that heavy orange bill.

❋

The down
i pluck from the
neck of the curlew
eddies and whirls at my knees
in the twilight wind
from sea.
kneeling in sand

warm in the hand.

�֎

"Do you want to do it right? I'll tell you."
he tells me.
at the edge of the water on the stones.
a transverse cut just below the sternum
the forefinger and middle finger
                forced in and up, following the
                curve of the rib cage.
then fingers arched, drawn slowly down and back,
forcing all the insides up and out,
toward the palm and heel of the hand.
firm organs, well-placed, hot.
save the liver;
finally scouring back, toward the vent, the last of the
                large intestine.

the insides string out, begin to wave, in the lapping
                waters of the bay.
the bird has no feathers, head, or feet;
                he is empty inside.
the rich body muscle that he moved by, the wing-beating
                muscle
anchored to the blade-like high breast bone,
is what you eat.

✖

The black iron frying pan on the coals.
two birds singed in flame.
bacon, onion, and garlic
browning, then steaming with a lid
put the livers in,
half a bird apiece and bulghour
passed about the fire on metal plates.
dense firm flesh,

dark and rich,
  gathered news of skies and seas.

☀

at dawn
looking out from the dunes
no birds at all but
three curlew

  ker-lew!

  ker-lew!

pacing   and glancing   around.

  Baja: Bahía de Concepción, '69

TWO FAWNS THAT DIDN'T SEE
THE LIGHT THIS SPRING

A friend in a tipi in the
Northern Rockies went out
hunting white tail with a
.22 and creeped up on a few
day-bedded, sleeping, shot
what he thought was a buck.
"It was a doe, and she was
carrying a fawn."
He cured the meat without
salt; sliced it following the
grain.

A friend in the Nothern Sierra
hit a doe with her car. It
walked out calmly in the lights,
"And when we butchered her
there was a fawn—about so long—
so tiny—but all formed and right.
It had spots. And the little
hooves were soft and white."

TWO IMMORTALS

Sitting on a bench by the Rogue River, Oregon, looking at a landform map. Two older gents approached and one, with baseball cap, began to sing: "California Here I Come"—he must have seen the license. Asked me if I'd ever heard of Texas Slim. Yes. And he said the song "If I Had the Wings of an Angel" was his, had been writ by him, "I was in the penitentiary." "Let me shake your hand! That's a good song" I said, and he showed me his hand: faint blue traces of tattoo on the back, on the bent fingers. And if I hit you with this hand it's L-O-V-E. And if I hit you with this hand it's H-A-T-E.

His friend, in a red and black buffalo check jacket stuck his hand out, under my nose, missing the forefinger. "How'd I lose that!" "How?" "An axe!"

Texas Slim said "I'm just giving him a ride. Last year his wife died." The two ambled off, chuckling, as Kai and Gen came running back up from the banks of Rogue River, hands full of round river stones.

Looking at the map, it was the space inside the loop of the upper Columbia, eastern Washington plateau country. "Channelled Scablands."

RAIN IN ALLEGHANY

standing in the thunder-pouring
heavy drops of water
        —dusty summer—
drinking beer just after driving
all the way around the
        watershed of rivers

rocky slopes and bumpy cars
its a skinny awkward land
like a workt-out miner's hand
        & how we love it
have some beer and rain,
stopping on our way,
in Alleghany

Alleghany California, home of the Sixteen to One Mine.

AVOCADO

The Dharma is like an Avocado!
Some parts so ripe you can't believe it,
But it's good.
And other places hard and green
Without much flavor,
Pleasing those who like their eggs well-cooked.

And the skin is thin,
The great big round seed
In the middle,
Is your own Original Nature—
Pure and smooth,
Almost nobody ever splits it open
Or ever tries to see
If it will grow.

Hard and slippery,
It looks like
You should plant it—but then
It shoots out thru the
                fingers—
gets away.

WHAT STEPS

Disciple: "Why is there evil in the universe?"
Ramakrishna: "To thicken the plot."

What steps.
Philip shaving his head,
Keith looney,
Allen benign,
Dick in charge,
Not magic, not transcendence exactly
but—all created things are of the Mother—
or—the un-created
day by day
stepping in
to the power within.
                    What steps
In the starry night.
    Tārā's eyes
    revolvers clicking
    raccoon eyes shine back
    lanterns fading
            (Bhagavan Das like a National Park)
    putting chains on
    in the mud.

To turn our mad dance partner spinning laughing
    ashes, ashes,
    —all fall down.

WHY LOG TRUCK DRIVERS RISE
EARLIER THAN STUDENTS OF ZEN

In the high seat, before-dawn dark,
Polished hubs gleam
And the shiny diesel stack
Warms and flutters
Up the Tyler Road grade
To the logging on Poorman creek.
Thirty miles of dust.

There is no other life.

◦ BEDROCK

for Masa

Snowmelt pond   warm granite
we make camp,
no thought of finding more.
and nap
and leave our minds to the wind.

on the bedrock, gently tilting,
sky and stone,

teach me to be tender.

the touch that nearly misses—
brush of glances—
tiny steps—
that finally cover worlds
        of hard terrain.
cloud wisps and mists
gathered into slate blue
bolts of summer rain.

tea together in the purple starry eve;
new moon soon to set,
why does it take so
long to learn to
love,
        we laugh
                and grieve.

THE DAZZLE
for Richard and Michael

the dazzle, the seduction the
design
intoxicated and quivering,
bees? is it flowers? why does this
seed move around.
the one
divides itself, divides, and divides again.
"we all know where that leads"
blinding storms of gold pollen.
—grope through that?
the dazzle
and the blue clay.
"all that moves, loves to sing"
the roots are at work.
unseen.

"ONE SHOULD NOT TALK TO A SKILLED HUNTER ABOUT WHAT IS FORBIDDEN BY THE BUDDHA"

—Hsiang-yen

A gray fox, female, nine pounds three ounces.
39 5/8″ long with tail.
Peeling skin back (Kai
reminded us to chant the *Shingyo* first)
cold pelt. crinkle; and musky smell
mixed with dead-body odor starting.

Stomach content: a whole ground squirrel well chewed
plus one lizard foot
and somewhere from inside the ground squirrel
a bit of aluminum foil.

The secret.
and the secret hidden deep in that.

LMFBR

Death himself,
      (Liquid Metal Fast Breeder Reactor)
      stands grinning, beckoning.
Plutonium tooth-glow.
Eyebrows buzzing.
Strip-mining scythe.

Kālī dances on the dead stiff cock.

      Aluminum beer cans, plastic spoons,
plywood veneer, PVC pipe, vinyl seat covers,
          don't exactly burn, don't quite rot,
          flood over us,

         robes and garbs
         of the Kālī-yūga

           end of days.

WALKING HOME FROM
"THE DUCHESS OF MALFI"

Walking home from "The Duchess of Malfi"
Bellatrix and Rigel gleam out of deep pits
Torn in the sea-cloud
          blown east from the Golden Gate

Months in the cabin: rain,
    cold, hard floor, leaking roof
    beautiful walls and windows—
        feeding birds

      once I
Struck and bit on thought
Of *being*
Being suffering,
Fought free, tearing hook and line
          (my mind)—
Thus was taught,
Pains of death and love,
Birth and war,
      wreckt earth,

      bless
With more love,

      not less.

Berkeley: 55

MAGPIE'S SONG

Six A.M.,
Sat down on excavation gravel
by juniper and desert S.P. tracks
interstate 80 not far off
    between trucks
Coyotes—maybe three
       howling and yapping from a rise.

Magpie on a bough
Tipped his head and said,

> *"Here in the mind, brother*
> *Turquoise blue.*
> *I wouldn't fool you.*
> *Smell the breeze*
> *It came through all the trees*
> *No need to fear*
> *What's ahead*
> *Snow up on the hills west*
> *Will be there every year*
> *be at rest.*
> *A feather on the ground—*
> *The wind sound—*

Here in the Mind, Brother,
Turquoise Blue"

FOR THE CHILDREN

O WATERS

        O waters
      wash us, me,
under the wrinkled granite
      straight-up slab,

and sitting by camp in the pine shade
Nanao sleeping,
mountains humming and crumbling
      snowfields melting
      soil
      building on tiny ledges
for wild onions and the flowers
            Blue
      Polemonium

            great
            earth
            sangha

GEN

Gen
little frown
buried in her breast
    and long black hair
Gen for milk
Gen for sleep
Gen for looking-over-shoulder
far beyond the waving eucalyptus
    limbs and farther dreaming crow
flying slow and steady for the ocean;
eyes over drippy nipple
    at the rising shadow sun
whales of cool and dark,
Gen patted-on-the-head by Kai,
"don't cry"

DUSTY BRACES

O you ancestors
lumber schooners
   big moustache
long-handled underwear
sticks out under the cuffs

tan stripes on each shoulder,
dusty braces—
  nine bows
  nine bows
you bastards
my fathers
and grandfathers, stiff-necked
punchers, miners, dirt farmers, railroad-men

killd off the cougar and grizzly

nine bows. Your itch
in my boots too,

—your sea roving
tree hearted son.

THE JEMEZ PUEBLO RING

Lost in the cracks of the walls or floors in Kyoto
Fell through and missed and sifted out
   when the house was razed,
Foundations poured and apartments raised above it—

In forty years the apartments useless and torn down,
   scrap wood burned for cooking and
   bath fires—

Another sixty passes, the land is good;
With an ox they snake off concrete shards—

On the tines of the fork
   in the black soil
   the crusted ring.
   wiped with the thumb
   turquoise stone still blue.

The expert looked at it and said,
   this is a ring from the century past.
   when there was travel and trade.
   from across the sea, east,

Silver, and blue of the desert sky.
   the style is old.
   though we never see them now,

Those corn-growing black-haired villagers
   are still there, making such rings,
   I'm told—

TOMORROW'S SONG

The USA slowly lost its mandate
in the middle and later twentieth century
it never gave the mountains and rivers,
      trees and animals,
        a vote.
all the people turned away from it
      myths die; even continents are impermanent

     Turtle Island returned.
     my friend broke open a dried coyote-scat
     removed a ground squirrel tooth
     pierced it, hung it
     from the gold ring
     in his ear.

We look to the future with pleasure
we need no fossil fuel
get power within
grow strong on less.

Grasp the tools and move in rhythm side by side
     flash gleams of wit and silent knowledge
        eye to eye
sit still like cats or snakes or stones
     as whole and holding as
        the blue black sky.
gentle and innocent as wolves
       as tricky as a prince.

At work and in our place:

    in the service
    of the wilderness
    of life
    of death
    of the Mother's breasts!

WHAT HAPPENED HERE BEFORE

-300,000,000-

First a sea: soft sands, muds, and marls
    —loading, compressing, heating, crumpling,
      crushing, recrystallizing, infiltrating,
several times lifted and submerged.
intruding molten granite magma
    deep-cooled and speckling,
      gold quartz fills the cracks—

-80,000,000-

sea-bed strata raised and folded,
    granite far below.
warm quiet centuries of rains
    (make dark red tropic soils)
      wear down two miles of surface,
lay bare the veins and tumble heavy gold
    in steambeds
      slate and schist rock-riffles catch it—
volcanic ash floats down and dams the streams,
    piles up the gold and gravel—

-3,000,000-

flowing north, two rivers joined,
    to make a wide long lake.
and then it tilted and the rivers fell apart
    all running west
      to cut the gorges of the Feather,
        Bear, and Yuba.

Ponderosa pine, manzanita, black oak, mountain yew.
        deer, coyote, bluejay, gray squirrel,
    ground squirrel, fox, blacktail hare,
        ringtail, bobcat, bear,
            all came to live here.

            −40,000−

And human people came with basket hats and nets
        winter-houses underground
        yew bows painted green,
        feasts and dances for the boys and girls
            songs and stories in the smoky dark.

            −125−

Then came the white man: tossed up trees and
        boulders with big hoses,
        going after that old gravel and the gold.
horses, apple-orchards, card-games,
        pistol-shooting, churches, county jail.

We asked, who the land belonged to.
        and where one pays tax.
(two gents who never used it twenty years,
and before them the widow
        of the son of the man
        who got him a patented deed
        on a worked-out mining claim,)
laid hasty on land that was deer and acorn
        grounds of the Nisenan?
        branch of the Maidu?

(they never had a chance to speak, even,
        their name.)
(and who remembers the Treaty of Guadalupe Hidalgo.)

        the land belongs to itself.
        "no self in self; no self in things"

        Turtle Island swims
        in the ocean-sky swirl-void
        biting its tail while the worlds go
                on-and-off
                winking

& Mr. Tobiassen, a Cousin Jack,
        assesses the county tax.
(the tax is our body-mind, guest at the banquet
        Memorial and Annual, in honor
        of sunlight grown heavy and tasty
        while moving up food-chains
in search of a body with eyes and a fairly large
        brain—
        to look back at itself
        on high.)

                now,

we sit here near the diggings
in the forest, by our fire, and watch
the moon and planets and the shooting stars—

my sons ask, who are we?
drying apples picked from homestead trees
drying berries, curing meat,
shooting arrows at a bale of straw.

military jets head northeast, roaring, every dawn.

my sons ask, who are they?

> *WE SHALL SEE*
> *WHO KNOWS*
> *HOW TO BE*

Bluejay screeches from a pine.

TOWARD CLIMAX

I.

salt seas, mountains, deserts—
cell mandala holding water
nerve network linking toes and eyes
fins   legs   wings—
teeth, all-purpose little early mammal molars.
primate flat-foot
front fore-mounted eyes—

watching at the forest-grassland (interface
richness) edge.
scavenge, gather, rise up on rear legs.
running—grasping—hand and eye;
hunting.
calling others to the stalk, the drive.

note sharp points of split bone; broken rock.

brain-size blossoming
on the balance of the neck,
tough skin—good eyes—sharp ears—
move in bands.
milkweed fiber rolled out on the thigh;
       nets to carry fruits or meat.

catch fire, move on.
eurasia tundra reindeer herds
sewn hide clothing, mammoth-rib-framework tent.

Bison, bear,   skinned and split;
    opening animal chests and bellies, skulls,
    bodies just like ours—
pictures in caves.

send sound off the mouth and lips
formal complex grammars transect
        inner structures & the daily world—

big herds dwindle
        (—did we kill them?
        thousand-mile front of prairie fire—)
ice age warms up
learn more plants. netting, trapping, boats.
bow and arrow. dogs.
mingle bands and families in and out like language
        kin to grubs and trees and wolves

        dance and sing.
begin to go "beyond"—   reed flute—
        buried baby wrapped in many furs—
great dream-time tales to tell.

squash blossom in the garbage heap.
        start farming.
cows won't stay away, start herding.
weaving, throwing clay.
get better off, get class,
make lists, start writing down.

        forget wild plants, their virtues
        lose dream-time
        lose largest size of brain—

get safer, tighter, wrapped in,
winding smaller, spreading wider,
lay towns out in streets in rows,
and build a wall.

drain swamp for wet-rice grasses, burn back woods,
herd men like cows.
have slaves build a fleet

raid for wealth—bronze weapons
horse and wagon—iron—war.

study stars and figure central
never-moving Pole Star King.

II.

From "King" project a Law. (Foxy self-
survival sense is Reason, since it "works")
and Reason gets ferocious as it goes for
order throughout nature—turns Law back on
nature. (A rooster was burned at the stake
for laying an egg. Unnatural. 1474.)

III.

science walks in beauty:

nets are many knots
skin is border-guard, a pelt is borrowed warmth;
a bow is the flex of a limb in the wind
a giant downtown building
        is a creekbed stood on end.

detritus pathways. "delayed and complex ways
to pass the food through webs."

maturity. stop and think. draw on the mind's
stored richness. memory, dream, half-digested
image of your life. "detritus pathways"—feed
the many tiny things that feed an owl.
send heart boldly travelling,
on the heat of the dead & down.

IV.

two logging songs

Clear-cut

Forestry. "How
Many people
Were harvested
In Viet-Nam?"

Clear-cut. "Some
Were children,
Some were over-ripe."

Virgin

A virgin
Forest
Is ancient; many-
Breasted,
Stable; at
Climax.

FOR THE CHILDREN

The rising hills, the slopes,
of statistics
lie before us.
the steep climb
of everything, going up,
up, as we all
go down.

In the next century
or the one beyond that,
they say,
are valleys, pastures,
we can meet there in peace
if we make it.

To climb these coming crests
one word to you, to
you and your children:

stay together
learn the flowers
go light

AS FOR POETS

As for poets
The Earth Poets
Who write small poems,
Need help from no man.

❋

The Air Poets
Play out the swiftest gales
And sometimes loll in the eddies.
Poem after poem,
Curling back on the same thrust.

❋

At fifty below
Fuel oil won't flow
And propane stays in the tank.
Fire Poets
Burn at absolute zero
Fossil love pumped back up.

❋

The first
Water Poet
Stayed down six years.
He was covered with seaweed.
The life in his poem
Left millions of tiny
Different tracks
Criss-crossing through the mud.

❋

With the Sun and Moon
In his belly,
The Space Poet
Sleeps.
No end to the sky—
But his poems,
Like wild geese,
Fly off the edge.

✻

A Mind Poet
Stays in the house.
The house is empty
And it has no walls.
The poem
Is seen from all sides,
Everywhere,
At once.

PLAIN TALK

FOUR CHANGES

Four Changes was written in the summer of '69 in response to an evident need for a few practical and visionary suggestions. Michael McClure, Richard Brautigan, Steve Beckwitt, Keith Lampe, Cliff Humphreys, Alan Watts, Allen Hoffman, Stewart Brand, and Diane de Prima were among those who read it during its formative period and offered suggestions and criticisms. It was printed and distributed widely, free, through the help of Alan Watts and Robert Shapiro. Several other free editions circulated, including one beautifully printed version by Noel Young of Santa Barbara. Far from perfect and in some parts already outdated, it may still be useful. Sections in brackets are recent commentary.

Whatever happens, we must not go into a plutonium-based economy. If the concept of a steady-state economy can be grasped and started in practice by say, 1980, we may be able to dodge the blind leap into the liquid metal fast breeder reactor—and extensive strip-mining—a path once entered, hard to turn back.

My Teacher once said to me,
  —become one with the knot itself,
    til it dissolves away.
  —sweep the garden.
  —any size.

I. POPULATION

The Condition

Position: Man is but a part of the fabric of life—dependent on the whole fabric for his very existence. As the most highly developed tool-using animal, he must recognize that the unknown evolutionary destinies of other life forms are to be respected, and act as gentle steward of the earth's community of being.

Situation: There are now too many human beings, and the problem is growing rapidly worse. It is potentially disastrous not only for the human race but for most other life forms.

Goal: The goal would be half of the present world population, or less.

Action

Social/political: First, a massive effort to convince the governments and leaders of the world that the problem is severe. And that all talk about raising food-production—well intentioned as it is—simply puts off the only real solution: reduce population. Demand immediate participation by all countries in programs to legalize abortion, encourage vasectomy and sterilization (provided by free clinics)—free insertion of intrauterine loops—try to correct traditional cultural attitudes that tend to force women into child-bearing—remove income tax deductions for more than two children above a specified income level, and scale it so that lower income families are forced to be careful too—or pay families to limit their number. Take a vigorous stand against the policy of the right wing in the Catholic hierarchy and any other institutions that exercise an irresponsible social force in regard to this question; oppose and correct simple-minded boosterism that equates population growth with continuing prosperity. Work ceaselessly to have all political questions be seen in the light of this prime problem.

[The governments are the wrong agents to address. Their most likely use of a problem, or crisis, is to seize it as another excuse for extending their own powers. Abortion should be legal and voluntary, but questions about vasectomy side-effects still come up. Great care should be taken that no one is ever tricked or forced into sterilization. The whole population issue is fraught with contradictions: but the fact stands that by standards of planetary biological welfare there are already too many human beings. The long-range answer is steady low birth rate. Area by area of the globe, the criteria of "optimum population" should be based on the sense of total ecological health for the region, including flourishing wildlife populations.]

The community: Explore other social structures and marriage forms, such as group marriage and polyandrous marriage, which provide family life but many less children. Share the pleasures of raising children widely, so that all need not directly reproduce to enter into this basic human experience. We must hope that no woman would give birth to more than one [two?] child, during this period of crisis. Adopt children. Let reverence for life and reverence for the feminine mean also a reverence for other species, and future human lives, most of which are threatened.

Our own heads: "I am a child of all life, and all living beings are my brothers and sisters, my children and grandchildren. And there is a child within me waiting to be brought to birth, the baby of a new and wiser self." Love, Love-making, a man and woman together, seen as the vehicle of mutual realization, where the creation of new selves and a new world of being is as important as reproducing our kind.

II.   POLLUTION

The Condition

Position: Pollution is of two types. One sort results from an excess of some fairly ordinary substance—smoke, or solid waste —which cannot be absorbed or transmitted rapidly enough to offset its introduction into the environment, thus causing changes the great cycle is not prepared for. (All organisms have wastes and by-products, and these are indeed part of the total biosphere: energy is passed along the line and refracted in various ways, "the rainbow body." This is cycling, not pollution.) The other sort is powerful modern chemicals and poisons, products of recent technology, which the biosphere is totally unprepared for. Such is DDT and similar chlorinated hydrocarbons—nuclear testing fall-out and nuclear waste—poison gas, germ and virus storage and leakage by the military; and chemicals which are put into food, whose long-range effects on human beings have not been properly tested.

Situation: The human race in the last century has allowed its production and scattering of wastes, by-products, and various chemicals to become excessive. Pollution is directly harming life on the planet: which is to say, ruining the environment for humanity itself. We are fouling our air and water, and living in noise and filth that no "animal" would tolerate, while advertising and politicians try and tell us we've never had it so good. The dependence of the modern governments on this kind of untruth leads to shameful mind-pollution: mass media and much school education.

Goal: Clean air, clean clear-running rivers, the presence of Pelican and Osprey and Gray Whale in our lives; salmon and trout in our streams; unmuddied language and good dreams.

Action

Social/political: Effective international legislation banning DDT and other poisons—with no fooling around. The collusion of certain scientists with the pesticide industry and agri-business in trying to block this legislation must be brought out in the open. Strong penalties for water and air pollution by industries—"Pollution is somebody's profit." Phase out the internal combustion engine and fossil fuel use in general—more research into non-polluting energy sources; solar energy; the tides. No more kidding the public about nuclear waste disposal: it's impossible to do it safely, and nuclear-generated electricity cannot be seriously planned for as it stands now. [Energy: we know a lot more about this problem now. Non-polluting energy resources such as solar or tides, would be clearly inadequate to supply the power needs of the world techno-industrial cancer. Five hundred years of strip-mining is not acceptable.

94

To go into the liquid metal fast breeder reactor on the gamble that we'll come out with the fusion process perfected is not acceptable. Research should continue on nuclear power, but divorced from any crash-program mentality. This means, conserve energy. "Do more with less." "Convert Waste into Treasure."] Stop all germ and chemical warfare research and experimentation; work toward a hopefully safe disposal of the present staggering and stupid stockpiles of H-bombs, cobalt gunk, germ and poison tanks and cans. Laws and sanctions against wasteful use of paper etc. which adds to the solid wastes of cities—develop methods of recycling solid urban wastes. Recycling should be the basic principle behind all waste-disposal thinking. Thus, all bottles should be reusable; old cans should make more cans; old newspapers back into newsprint again. Stronger controls and research on chemicals in foods. A shift toward a more varied and sensitive type of agriculture (more small-scale and subsistence farming) would eliminate much of the call for blanket use of pesticides.

The community: DDT and such: don't use them. Air pollution: use less cars. Cars pollute the air, and one or two people riding lonely in a huge car is an insult to intelligence and the Earth. Share rides, legalize hitch-hiking, and build hitch-hiker waiting stations along the highways. Also—a step toward the new world—walk more; look for the best routes through beautiful countryside for long-distance walking trips: San Francisco to Los Angeles down the Coast Range, for example. Learn how to use your own manure as fertilizer if you're in the country—as the Far East has done for centuries. There's a way, and it's safe. Solid waste: boycott bulky wasteful Sunday papers which use up trees. It's all just advertising anyway, which is artificially inducing more energy consumption. Refuse paper bags at the store. Organize Park and Street clean-up festivals. Don't work in any way for or with an industry which pollutes, and don't be drafted into the military. Don't waste. (A monk and an old master were once walking in the mountains. They noticed a little hut upstream. The monk said, "A wise hermit must live there"—the master said, "That's no wise hermit, you see that lettuce leaf floating down the stream, he's a Waster." Just then an old man came running down the hill with his beard flying and caught the floating lettuce leaf.) Carry your own jug to the winery and have it filled from the barrel.

Our own heads: Part of the trouble with talking about something like DDT is that the use of it is not just a practical devise, it's almost an establishment religion. There is something in Western culture that wants to totally wipe out creepy-crawlies, and feels repugnance for toadstools and snakes. This is fear of one's own deepest natural inner-self wilderness areas, and the answer is, relax. Relax around bugs, snakes, and your own hairy dreams. Again, we all should share our crops with a certain percentage of buglife as "paying our dues." Thoreau says: "How then can the harvest fail? Shall I not rejoice also at the abundance of the weeds whose seeds are the granary of the birds? It matters little comparatively whether the fields fill the farmer's barns. The true husbandman will cease from anxiety, as the squirrels manifest no concern whether the woods will bear chestnuts this year or not, and finish his labor with every day, relinquish all claim to the produce of his fields, and sacrificing in his mind not only his first but his last fruits also." In the realm of thought, inner experience, consciousness, as in the outward realm of interconnection, there is a difference between balanced cycle, and the excess which cannot be handled. When the balance is right, the mind recycles from highest illuminations to the muddy blinding anger or grabbiness which sometimes seizes us all; the alchemical "transmutation."

III. CONSUMPTION

The Condition

Position: Everything that lives eats food, and is food in turn.

This complicated animal, man, rests on a vast and delicate pyramid of energy-transformations. To grossly use more than you need, to destroy, is biologically unsound. Much of the production and consumption of modern societies is not necessary or conducive to spiritual and cultural growth, let alone survival; and is behind much greed and envy, age-old causes of social and international discord.

Situation: Man's careless use of "resources" and his total dependence on certain substances such as fossil fuels (which are being exhausted, slowly but certainly) are having harmful effects on all the other members of the life-network. The complexity of modern technology renders whole populations vulnerable to the deadly consequences of the loss of any one key resource. Instead of independence we have overdependence on life-giving substances such as water, which we squander. Many species of animals and birds have become extinct in the service of fashion fads—or fertilizer—or industrial oil—the soil is being used up; in fact mankind has become a locustlike blight on the planet that will leave a bare cupboard for its own children— all the while in a kind of Addict's Dream of affluence, comfort, eternal progress—using the great achievements of science to produce software and swill.

Goal: Balance, harmony, humility, growth which is a mutual growth with Redwood and Quail; to be a good member of the great community of living creatures. True affluence is not needing anything.

Action

Social/political: It must be demonstrated ceaselessly that a continually "growing economy" is no longer healthy, but a Cancer. And that the criminal waste which is allowed in the name of competition—especially that ultimate in wasteful needless competition, hot wars and cold wars with "Communism" (or "Capitalism")—must be halted totally with ferocious energy and decision. Economics must be seen as a small sub-branch of Ecology, and production/distribution/consumption handled by companies or unions or co-operatives, with the same elegance and spareness one sees in nature. Soil banks; open spaces; [logging to be truly based on sustained yield; the U.S. Forest Service is—sadly—now the lackey of business.] Protection for all scarce predators and varmints: "Support your right to arm bears." Damn the International Whaling Commission which is selling out the last of our precious, wise whales; absolutely no further development of roads and concessions in National Parks and Wilderness Areas; build auto campgrounds in the least desirable areas. Consumer boycotts in response to dishonest and unnecessary products. Radical Co-ops. Politically, blast both "Communist" and "Capitalist" myths of progress, and all crude notions of conquering or controlling nature.

The community: Sharing and creating. The inherent aptness of communal life—where large tools are owned jointly and used efficiently. The power of renunciation: If enough Americans refused to buy a new car for one given year, it would permanently alter the American economy. Recycling clothes and equipment. Support handicrafts, gardening, home skills, midwifery, herbs—all the things that can make us independent, beautiful and whole. Learn to break the habit of unnecessary possessions—a monkey on everybody's back—but avoid a self-abnegating anti-joyous self-righteousness. Simplicity is light, carefree, neat and loving—not a self-punishing ascetic trip. (The great Chinese poet Tu Fu said, "The ideas of a poet should be noble and simple.") Don't shoot a deer if you don't know how to use all the meat and preserve that which you can't eat, to tan the hide and use the leather—to use it all, with gratitude, right down to the sinew and hooves. Simplicity and mindfulness in diet is a starting point for many people.

Our own heads: It is hard to even begin to guage how much a complication of possessions, the notions of "my and mine," stand between us and a true, clear, liberated way of seeing

98

the world. To live lightly on the earth, to be aware and alive, to be free of egotism, to be in contact with plants and animals, starts with simple concrete acts. The inner principle is the insight that we are interdependent energy-fields of great potential wisdom and compassion—expressed in each person as a superb mind, a handsome and complex body, and the almost magical capacity of language. To these potentials and capacities, "owning things" can add nothing of authenticity. "Clad in the sky, with the earth for a pillow."

IV.   TRANSFORMATION

The Condition

Position: Everyone is the result of four forces: the conditions of this known-universe (matter/energy forms and ceaseless change); the biology of his species; his individual genetic heritage and the culture he's born into. Within this web of forces there are certain spaces and loops which allow to some persons the experience of inner freedom and illumination. The gradual exploration of some of these spaces is "evolution" and, for human cultures, what "history" could increasingly be. We have it within our deepest powers not only to change our "selves" but to change our culture. If man is to remain on earth he must transform the five-millenia-long urbanizing civilization tradition into a new ecologically-sensitive harmony-oriented wild-minded scientific-spiritual culture. "Wildness is the state of complete awareness. That's why we need it."

Situation: Civilization, which has made us so successful a species, has overshot itself and now threatens us with its inertia. There also is some evidence that civilized life isn't good for the human gene pool. To achieve the Changes we must change the very foundations of our society and our minds.

Goal: Nothing short of total transformation will do much good. What we envision is a planet on which the human population lives harmoniously and dynamically by employing various sophisticated and unobtrusive technologies in a world environment which is "left natural." Specific points in this vision:

—A healthy and spare population of all races, much less in number than today.

—Cultural and individual pluralism, unified by a type of world tribal council. Division by natural and cultural boundaries rather than arbitrary political boundaries.

—A technology of communication, education, and quiet transportation, land-use being sensitive to the properties of each region. Allowing, thus, the Bison to return to much of the high plains. Careful but intensive agriculture in the great alluvial valleys; deserts left wild for those who would live there by skill. Computer technicians who run the plant part of the year and walk along with the Elk in their migrations during the rest.

—A basic cultural outlook and social organization that inhibits power and property-seeking while encouraging exploration and challenge in things like music, meditation, mathematics, mountaineering, magic, and all other ways of authentic being-in-the-world. Women totally free and equal. A new kind of family—responsible, but more festive and relaxed—is implicit.

Action

Social/political: It seems evident that there are throughout the world certain social and religious forces which have worked through history toward an ecologically and culturally enlightened state of affairs. Let these be encouraged: Gnostics, hip Marxists, Teilhard de Chardin Catholics, Druids, Taoists, Biologists, Witches, Yogins, Bhikkus, Quakers, Sufis, Tibetans, Zens, Shamans, Bushmen, American Indians, Polynesians, Anarchists, Alchemists . . . the list is long. Primitive cultures, communal and ashram movements, co-operative ventures.

Since it doesn't seem practical or even desirable to think that direct bloody force will achieve much, it would be best to consider this a continuing "revolution of consciousness" which will be won not by guns but by seizing the key images, myths, archetypes, eschatologies, and ecstasies so that life won't seem worth living unless one's on the transforming energy's side. We must take over "science and technology" and release its real possibilities and powers in the service of this planet—which, after all produced us and it.

[More concretely: no transformation without our feet on the ground. Stewardship means, for most of us, find your place on the planet, dig in, and take responsibility from there—the tiresome but tangible work of school boards, county supervisors, local foresters—local politics. Even while holding in mind the largest scale of potential change. Get a sense of workable territory, learn about it, and start acting point by point. On all levels from national to local the need to move toward steady state economy—equilibrium, dynamic balance, inner-growth stressed—must be taught. Maturity/diversity/climax/creativity.]

The community: New schools, new classes, walking in the woods and cleaning up the streets. Find psychological techniques for creating an awareness of "self" which includes the social and natural environment. "Consideration of what specific language forms—symbolic systems—and social institutions constitute obstacles to ecological awareness." Without falling into a facile interpretation of McLuhan, we can hope to use the media. Let no one be ignorant of the facts of biology and related disciplines; bring up our children as part of the wildlife. Some communities can establish themselves in backwater rural areas and flourish—others maintain themselves in urban centers, and the two types work together—a two-way flow of experience, people, money and home-grown vegetables. Ultimately cities may exist only as joyous tribal gatherings and fairs, to dissolve after a few weeks. Investigating new life-styles is our work, as is the exploration of Ways to explore our inner realms—with the known dangers of crashing that go with such.

101

Master the archaic and the primitive as models of basic nature-related cultures—as well as the most imaginative extensions of science—and build a community where these two vectors cross.

Our own heads: Is where it starts. Knowing that we are the first human beings in history to have so much of man's culture and previous experience available to our study, and being free enough of the weight of traditional cultures to seek out a larger identity; the first members of a civilized society since the Neolithic to wish to look clearly into the eyes of the wild and see our self-hood, our family, there. We have these advantages to set off the obvious disadvantages of being as screwed up as we are—which gives us a fair chance to penetrate some of the riddles of ourselves and the universe, and to go beyond the idea of "man's survival" or "survival of the biosphere" and to draw our strength from the realization that at the heart of things is some kind of serene and ecstatic process which is beyond qualities and beyond birth-and-death. "No need to survive!" "In the fires that destroy the universe at the end of the kalpa, what survives?"—"The iron tree blooms in the void!"

Knowing that nothing need be done, is where we begin to move from.

"ENERGY IS ETERNAL DELIGHT"

A young woman at Sir George Williams University in Montreal asked me, "What do you fear most?" I found myself answering "that the diversity and richness of the gene pool will be destroyed—" and most people there understood what was meant.

The treasure of life is the richness of stored information in the diverse genes of all living beings. If the human race, following on some set of catastrophes, were to survive at the expense of many plant and animal species, it would be no victory. Diversity provides life with the capacity for a multitude of adaptations and responses to long-range changes on the planet. The possibility remains that at some future time another evolutionary line might carry the development of consciousness to clearer levels than our family of upright primates.

The United States, Europe, the Soviet Union, and Japan have a habit. They are addicted to heavy energy use, great gulps and injections of fossil fuel. As fossil-fuel reserves go down, they will take dangerous gambles with the future health of the biosphere (through nuclear power) to keep up their habit.

For several centuries Western civilization has had a priapic drive for material accumulation, continual extensions of political and economic power, termed "progress." In the Judaeo-Christian worldview men are seen as working out their ultimate destinies (paradise? perdition?) with planet earth as the stage for the drama—trees and animals mere props, nature a vast supply depot. Fed by fossil fuel, this religio-economic view has become a cancer: uncontrollable growth. It may finally choke itself, and drag much else down with it.

The longing for growth is not wrong. The nub of the problem now is how to flip over, as in jujitsu, the magnificent growth-energy of modern civilization into a nonacquisitive search for deeper knowledge of self and nature. Self-nature. Mother nature. If people come to realize that there are many nonmaterial, nondestructive paths of growth—of the highest and most fascinating order—it would help dampen the common fear that a steady state economy would mean deadly stagnation.

I spent a few years, some time back, in and around a training place. It was a school for monks of the Rinzai branch of Zen Buddhism, in Japan. The whole aim of the community was personal and universal liberation. In this quest for spiritual freedom every man marched strictly to the same drum in matters of hours of work and meditation. In the teacher's room one was pushed across sticky barriers into vast new spaces. The training was traditional and had been handed down for centuries—but the insights are forever fresh and new. The beauty, refinement and truly civilized quality of that life has no match in modern America. It is supported by hand labor in small fields, gathering brushwood to heat the bath, wellwater and barrels of homemade pickles. The unspoken motto is "Grow With Less." In the training place I lost my remaining doubts about China.

The Buddhists teach respect for all life, and for wild systems. Man's life is totally dependent on an interpenetrating network of wild systems. Eugene Odum, in his useful paper "The Strategy of Ecosystem Development," points out how the United States has the characteristics of a young ecosystem. Some American Indian cultures have "mature" characteristics: protection as against production, stability as against growth, quality as against quantity. In Pueblo societies a kind of ultimate democracy is practiced. Plants and animals are also people, and, through certain rituals and dances, are given a place and a voice in the political discussions of the humans. They are "represented." "Power to all the people" must be the slogan.

On Hopi and Navajo land, at Black Mesa, the whole issue is revolving at this moment. The cancer is eating away at the breast of Mother Earth in the form of strip-mining. This to provide electricity for Los Angeles. The defense of Black Mesa is being sustained by traditional Indians, young Indian militants, and longhairs. Black Mesa speaks to us through an ancient, complex web of myth. She is sacred territory. To hear her voice is to give up the European word "America" and accept the new-old name for the continent, "Turtle Island."

The return to marginal farmland on the part of longhairs is not some nostalgic replay of the nineteenth century. Here is a generation of white people finally ready to learn from the Elders. How to live on the continent as though our children, and on down, for many ages, will still be here (not on the moon). Loving and protecting this soil, these trees, these wolves. Natives of Turtle Island.

A scaled-down, balanced technology is possible, if cut loose from the cancer of exploitation-heavy-industry-perpetual growth. Those who have already sensed these necessities and have begun, whether in the country or the city, to "grow with less," are the only counterculture that counts. Electricity for Los Angeles is not energy. As Blake said: "Energy Is Eternal Delight."

THE WILDERNESS

I am a poet. My teachers are other poets, American Indians, and a few Buddhist priests in Japan. The reason I am here is because I wish to bring a voice from the wilderness, my constituency. I wish to be a spokesman for a realm that is not usually represented either in intellectual chambers or in the chambers of government.

I was climbing Glacier Peak in the Cascades of Washington several years ago, on one of the clearest days I had ever seen. When we reached the summit of Glacier Peak we could see almost to the Selkirks in Canada. We could see south far beyond the Columbia River to Mount Hood and Mount Jefferson. And, of course, we could see Mount Adams and Mount Rainier. We could see across Puget Sound to the ranges of the Olympic Mountains. My companion, who is a poet, said: "You mean, there is a senator for all this?"

Unfortunately, there isn't a senator for all that. And I would like to think of a new definition of humanism and a new definition of democracy that would include the nonhuman, that would have representation from those spheres. This is what I think we mean by an ecological conscience.

I don't like Western culture because I think it has much in it that is inherently wrong and that is at the root of the environmental crisis that is not recent; it is very ancient; it has been building up for a millennium. There are many things in Western culture that are admirable. But a culture that alienates itself from the very ground of its own being—from the wilderness outside (that is to say, wild nature, the wild, self-contained, self-informing ecosystems) and from that other wilderness, the wilderness within—is doomed to a very destructive behavior, ultimately perhaps self-destructive behavior.

The West is not the only culture that carries these destructive seeds. China had effectively deforested itself by 1000 A.D.

Transcript of a statement made at a seminar at The Center for the Study of Democratic Institutions, Santa Barbara, California.

India had effectively deforested itself by 800 A.D. The soils of the Middle East were ruined even earlier. The forests that once covered the mountains of Yugoslavia were stripped to build the Roman fleet, and those mountains have looked like Utah ever since. The soils of southern Italy and Sicily were ruined by latifundia slave-labor farming in the Roman Empire. The soils of the Atlantic seaboard in the United States were effectively ruined before the American Revolution because of the one-crop (tobacco) farming. So the same forces have been at work in East and West.

You would not think a poet would get involved in these things. But the voice that speaks to me as a poet, what Westerners have called the Muse, is the voice of nature herself, whom the ancient poets called the great goddess, the Magna Mater. I regard that voice as a very real entity. At the root of the problem where our civilization goes wrong is the mistaken belief that nature is something less than authentic, that nature is not as alive as man is, or as intelligent, that in a sense it is dead, and that animals are of so low an order of intelligence and feeling, we need not take their feelings into account.

A line is drawn between primitive peoples and civilized peoples. I think there is a wisdom in the worldview of primitive peoples that we have to refer ourselves to, and learn from. If we are on the verge of postcivilization, then our next step must take account of the primitive worldview which has traditionally and intelligently tried to open and keep open lines of communication with the forces of nature. You cannot communicate with the forces of nature in the laboratory. One of the problems is that we simply do not know much about primitive people and primitive cultures. If we can tentatively accommodate the possibility that nature has a degree of authenticity and intelligence that requires that we look at it more sensitively, then we can move to the next step. "Intelligence" is not really the right word. The ecologist Eugene Odum uses the term "biomass."

Life-biomass, he says, is stored information; living matter is stored information in the cells and in the genes. He believes there is more information of a higher order of sophistication and complexity stored in a few square yards of forest than there is in all the libraries of mankind. Obviously, that is a different order of information. It is the information of the universe we live in. It is the information that has been flowing for millions of years. In this total information context, man may not be necessarily the highest or most interesting product.

Perhaps one of its most interesting experiments at the point of evolution, if we can talk about evolution in this way, is not man but a high degree of biological diversity and sophistication opening to more and more possibilities. Plants are at the bottom of the food chain; they do the primary energy transformation that makes all the life-forms possible. So perhaps plant-life is what the ancients meant by the great goddess. Since plants support the other life-forms, they became the "people" of the land. And the land—a country—is a region within which the interactions of water, air, and soil and the underlying geology and the overlying (maybe stratospheric) wind conditions all go to create both the microclimates and the large climactic patterns that make a whole sphere or realm of life possible. The people in that realm include animals, humans, and a variety of wild life.

What we must find a way to do, then, is incorporate the other people—what the Sioux Indians called the creeping people, and the standing people, and the flying people, and the swimming people—into the councils of government. This isn't as difficult as you might think. If we don't do it, they will revolt against us. They will submit non-negotiable demands about our stay on the earth. We are beginning to get non-negotiable demands right now from the air, the water, the soil.

I would like to expand on what I mean by representation here at the Center from these other fields, these other societies, these other communities. Ecologists talk about the ecology of oak communities, or pine communities. They *are* communities. This institute—this Center—is of the order of a kiva of elders. Its function is to maintain and transmit the lore of the tribe on the highest levels. If it were doing its job completely, it would have a cycle of ceremonies geared to the seasons, geared perhaps to the migrations of the fish and to the phases of the moon. It would be able to instruct in what rituals you follow when a child is born, when someone reaches puberty, when someone gets married, when someone dies. But, as you know, in these fragmented times, one council cannot perform all these functions at one time. Still it would be understood that a council of elders, the caretakers of the lore of the culture, would open themselves to representation from other life-forms. Historically this has been done through art. The paintings of bison and bears in the caves of southern France were of that order. The animals were speaking through the people and making their point. And when, in the dances of the Pueblo Indians and other peoples, certain individuals became seized, as it were, by the spirit of the deer, and danced as a deer would dance, or danced the dance of the corn maidens, or impersonated the squash blossom, they were no longer speaking for humanity, they were taking it on themselves to interpret, through their humanity, what these other life-forms were. That is about all we know so far concerning the possibilities of incorporating spokesmanship for the rest of life in our democratic society.

Let me describe how a friend of mine from a Rio Grande pueblo hunts. He is twenty-seven years old. The Pueblo Indians, and I think probably most of the other Indians of the Southwest, begin their hunt, first, by purifying themselves. They take emetics, a sweat bath, and perhaps avoid their wife for a few days. They also try not to think certain thoughts. They go out hunting in an attitude of humility. They make sure that they need to hunt, that they are not hunting without necessity. Then they improvise a song while they are in the mountains. They sing aloud or hum to themselves while they are walking along. It is a song to the deer, asking the deer to be willing to die for them. They usually still-hunt, taking a place alongside a trail. The feeling is that you are not hunting the deer, the deer is coming to you; you make yourself available for the deer that will present itself to you, that has given itself to you. Then you shoot it. After you shoot it, you cut the head off and place the head facing east. You sprinkle corn meal in front of the mouth of the deer, and you pray to the deer, asking it to forgive you for having killed it, to understand that we all need to eat, and to please make a good report to the other deer spirits that he has been treated well. One finds this way of handling things and animals in all primitive cultures.

WHAT'S MEANT BY "HERE"

The gentle slopes and meadows of the lower ridge—fine deep groves that show what it once was all like, as on the Bureau of Land Management parcel soon to be logged by Yuba River Lumber Company, right next to Wepa land—and the shady, somewhat brushy, but calm and growing woods of the most of the ridge—a human space there. Enough room to fit a few two-legged beings in.

Crackly grass and Blue oak, the special smells of pungent sticky flowers, give way, climbing, through Digger pine and into Black oak and Ponderosa pine; sweet birch, manzanita, kitkitdizze. This is our home country. We dig wells and wonder where the water table comes from.

We wonder where the deer go in the summer heat, and where they come from in the fall. How far east into the high Sierra. In thirty steady climbing miles the ridge contacts the crest, eight thousand feet. Pure granite; little lakes. At zazen, 5:30 AM, the only sound beside the wind in the pines is the empty log-trucks groaning up Tyler road, across the old hydraulic-mining diggings, heading out from coffee-in-the-dark to timber sales far up the ridge in "checkerboard country"— Southern Pacific and Tahoe National Forest sections intermixed.

Down the hogsback little ridge from Chuck and Franco's place (we call it now; but a year ago, it was just "the grassy benches on the way to the river that you can see from the top of Bald Mountain—we looked for Lew Welch there, too") is a trail that was made on a Saturday community work day, a direct route down leading to the great hole and the right-angle bend of the South Fork of the Yuba, (named from Spanish *uva*, grapes). It is, just exactly, where the last clear string-of-bones of true Sierra Granite bares itself, and the river had to take notice of that hardness, she did, she made a bend.

We all went there one Monday in the summer with a rucksack of dinner picnic things and spent the afternoon at lazy swimming in the pippin-apple-green waters of the Yuba. Yuba Mā. Her Womb-Realm Mandala center right where we were, with only Bald Mountain (that ascetic) providing space for eyes upstream—rocky brushy slopes.

So, the ridge and the river. Back up again by dark. Under the pine and oak, three thousand feet, it's also cool. And only three miles from a mailbox.

Watershed: west slope of the northern Sierra Nevada, south slope of the east-west running ridge above the south fork, at the level of Black oak mixed with Ponderosa pine.

ON "AS FOR POETS"

"Energy is Eternal Delight"—William Blake, in *The Marriage of Heaven and Hell*. What are we to make of this? As the over-developed world (the U.S., Japan, etc.) approaches an "energy crisis" with shortages of oil and electric power (and some nations plan a desperate gamble with nuclear generating plants) we must remember that oil and coal are the stored energy of the sun locked by ancient plant-life in its cells. "Renewable" energy resources are the trees and flowers and all living beings of today, especially plant-life doing the primary work of energy-transfer.

On these fuels contemporary nations now depend. But there is another kind of energy, in every living being, close to the sun-source but in a different way. The power within. Whence? "Delight." The delight of being alive while knowing of impermanence and death, the acceptance and mastery of this. A definition:

Delight is the innocent joy arising
with the perception and realization of
the wonderful, empty, intricate,
inter-penetrating,
mutually-embracing, shining
single world beyond all discrimination
or opposites.*

* An alternative definition has been suggested by Dr. Edward Schafer of Berkeley, who describes himself as "an imaginative but unreasonable pedant" (but who is really a scholar of the prosody of artifacts, the poetry of tools).

Delight is the sophisticated joy arising
with the perception and realization of
the wonderful, replete, intricate,
rich-reflecting,
uniquely aloof, polychrome
complex worlds beyond all indifference
to nuances.

113

This joy is continually reflected in the poems and songs of the world. "As for Poets" explores the realm of delight in terms of the five elements that ancient Greek and China both saw as the constituents of the physical world. To which the Buddhist philosophers of India added a sixth, consciousness, or Mind. At one point I was tempted to title this poem "The Five Elements embracing; pierced by; Mind,"—as illustrated in the mūdra (hand position) generally seen on images of Vairocana Buddha (大日如来).

Earth is our Mother and a man or woman goes directly to her, needing no intermediary.

Air is our breath, spirit, inspiration; a flow which becomes speech when "sounded"—the curling back on the same thrust" is close to what is meant in the Japanese word *Fushi* (*bushi* 節)—knot, or whorl in the grain, the word for song.

Fire must have a fuel and the heart's fuel is love. The love that makes poetry burn is not just the green of this spring, but draws on the ancient web of sympathetic, compassionate, and erotic acts that lies behind our very existence, a stored energy in our genes and dreams—fossil love a sly term for that deep-buried sweetness brought to conscious thought.

Water is creation, the mud we crawled on; the wash of tides in the cells. The Water Poet is the Creator. His calligraphy is the trails and tracks we living beings leave in each other; in the world; his poem.

But swallow it all. Size is no problem, a little *space* encloses a huge void. There, those great whorls, the stars hang. Who can get outside the universe? But the poem was born elsewhere, and need not stay. Like the wild geese of the Arctic it heads home, far above the borders, where most things cannot cross.

Now, we are both in, and outside, the world at once. The only place this can be is the *Mind*. Ah, what a poem. It is what is, completely, in the past, present, and future simultaneously, seeing being, and being seen.

Can we really do this? But we do. So we sing. Poetry is for all men and women. The power within—the more you give, the more you have to give—will still be our source when coal and oil are long gone, and atoms are left to spin in peace.

114